THE KINDNESS MACHINE

WRITTEN BY
CHRISTINA DANKERT

ILLUSTRATED BY
CHAD DANKERT

Purple Butterfly Press

PURPLE BUTTERFLY PRESS
An Imprint of Kat Biggie Press
Columbia, SC
purplebutterflypress.net

DISCUSSION QUESTIONS

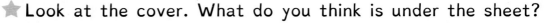

Before reading...

⭐ Look at the cover. What do you think is under the sheet?
⭐ What does it mean to be kind?
⭐ Give an example of a time you were kind to someone.
⭐ Give an example of a time someone was kind to you.

During reading...

⭐ Why do you think Mr. Wilson built the machine?
⭐ What examples of kindness are shown in the illustrations?
⭐ What kindness action would be the easiest to complete?
⭐ What kindness action would be the most challenging to complete?

After reading...

⭐ What is your superpower?
⭐ What was your favorite part of the story?
⭐ Why do you think the author wrote this book?
⭐ Give an example of how you can be kind to others.
⭐ Give an example of how you can be kind to yourself.

Publisher's Cataloging-In-Publication Data
(Prepared by The Donohue Group, Inc.)

Names: Dankert, Christina, author. | Dankert, Chad, illustrator.
Title: The kindness machine / written by Christina Dankert ; illustrated by Chad Dankert.
Description: First edition. | Columbia, SC : Purple Butterfly Press, [2022] | Includes discussion questions. | Interest age level: 003-008. | Summary: "Creative and artistic 2nd grade teacher, Mr. Wilson, is able to concretely provide examples of how his students can be kind. Mr. Wilson creates The Kindness Machine which is covered in idea buttons to demonstrate kind actions. Instead of telling his students to 'be kind,' which is something children hear from a very early age, they learn exact what they can do in their own lives by pressing the special buttons"--Provided by publisher.
Identifiers: ISBN 9781955119085 (hardback) | ISBN 9781955119092 (paperback) | ISBN 9781955119108 (ebook)
Subjects: LCSH: Kindness--Juvenile fiction. | Teachers--Juvenile fiction. | Children--Conduct of life--Juvenile fiction. | CYAC
  Kindness--Fiction. | Teachers--Fiction. | Conduct of life--Fiction.
Classification: LCC PZ7.1.D32 Ki 2022 (print) | LCC PZ7.1.D32 (ebook) | DDC [E]--dc23

Everyone in Tree City knew that Mr. Wilson
was the best second-grade teacher in town.
He was caring, energetic, and imaginative!
Mr. Wilson could often be found drawing
or building.

He enjoyed inventing new gadgets like his Super Zeller Speller or his Marvelous Math Machine.

He always found a way to bring his extraordinary inventions into his classroom.

One day, I walked into my classroom and noticed a bedsheet draped over something very large. Mr. Wilson, with a twinkle of excitement in his eyes, exclaimed, "Raise your hand if you have a superpower!"

Everyone looked around the room, but no one raised a hand. Mr. Wilson furrowed his eyebrows in surprise. "Why is no one raising a hand?" he asked.

My best friend, Connor, and I looked at each other and shrugged. I turned to Mr. Wilson and asked, "A superpower? Mr. Wilson, none of us can fly, be invisible, breathe underwater, or do anything a superhero can do."

Mr. Wilson laughed heartily. With a smile on his face, he said, "Cora, what if I told you that **ALL** of you have a superpower?"

He walked to the front of the classroom and placed his hand on the bedsheet. We all inched to the edge of our seats, waiting to see what was going to be revealed.

With a quick move of his hand, as if he were a magician revealing his greatest trick, he snatched the sheet away.

"*This* is the Kindness Machine," Mr. Wilson proudly stated.

We all sprang to our feet and rushed over to the gigantic machine. It was taller than Mr. Wilson, covered in buttons, and had a large screen at the top. The buttons were in every color and shape imaginable! There were levers all over and springs popping out on the sides.

Mr. Wilson said, "You have probably heard an adult tell you how important it is to be kind, but what does that mean and how can you do that? Today's lesson is all about how we can be kind, compassionate, and understanding to each other and ourselves. There are many ways you can do this, and each button gives you an example of how to practice kindness in the real world."

Mr. Wilson invited Mia to push the first button. Mia slowly stepped closer to the machine. Her eyes darted from the machine to Mr. Wilson in uncertainty. With a smile and a nod from Mr. Wilson, she hesitantly pushed a square pink button

The screen above the machine exploded with lights and colors and then displayed the kindness idea: "SMILE!"

Mr. Wilson beamed and then explained, "It doesn't matter how old you are; everyone can be kind. You can start by simply smiling at someone. Smiles are contagious, which means they are easily passed from one person to another. Try it!"

We slowly turned to one another, offering little smiles to our classmates. It didn't take long for our grins to widen and turn into larger smiles. Suddenly, as if we couldn't control it, we started giggling and then burst into laughter.

HOW CAN YOU MAKE SOMEONE SMILE?

Next, Mason excitedly stood up and pushed the triangular blue button. The words, "SAY IT!" appeared on the screen.

Mr. Wilson explained, "Another way to be kind is to compliment someone. We all know the saying, 'If you don't have anything nice to say, don't say anything at all.' But, if you do have something nice to say, be sure to say it! We often think of compliments in our heads but might not share them out loud. So be sure to spread your kindness compliment. It will make that person *and* you feel great!"

Connor waved his hand into the air, eager to have a turn at pushing a button. Mr. Wilson nodded in his direction and called him up. With confidence, he walked up and pushed the square tie-dye button. "**LOVE YOURSELF!**" appeared on the screen.

Mr. Wilson announced, "It is so important to be kind to others, but it is also important to be kind to yourself. What does this mean? For starters, you can talk positively to yourself. Instead of getting frustrated, tell yourself that you can do it. If you make a mistake, tell yourself that it's okay if you can't do something right away."

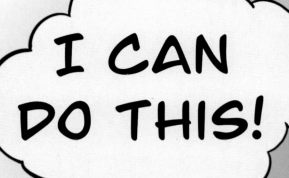

I CAN DO THIS!

"Just keep trying until you can. Always believe in yourself, know that you can do anything, and that you are amazing!"

I'M PROUD, I DID MY BEST!

WHAT DO YOU LOVE ABOUT YOURSELF?

By now, our class was excitedly chatting about all the kindness ideas. Lydia was so thrilled that she ran up and pushed two buttons!

Mr. Wilson shouted, "INVITE AND INCLUDE! Inviting someone to play with you or talking to someone new are two great ways to be kind. Everyone likes to feel included, so keep your eyes open for someone who looks like they could use a friend and *be* that friend."

Mr. Wilson announced that we had time for one more idea button. "Cora, will you please select the last button for today?" With a large smile on my face, I pushed the rainbow button.

Mr. Wilson burst with excitement and said, "Oh! I just love this one! **BE A CHEF!** Kindness is like baking a cake. The ideas from the Kindness Machine are your ingredients. Each kindness action is great on its own, but the real magic happens when you combine them. It is up to you to take the ideas and turn them into beautiful and wonderful kindness actions."

Cora's eyes widened as she realized, "Mr. Wilson, we have our own Kindness Machine inside us!"

Grinning, Mr. Wilson said, "You absolutely do! Your beautiful brain and heart will help guide you to be the best you can be as you practice kindness to others and to yourself. **SMILE, SAY IT, LOVE YOURSELF, INVITE AND INCLUDE,** and most importantly, **BE A CHEF** with those special ingredients. I invite you to look inside your own Kindness Machine and always choose to be kind."

INVITE AND INCLUDE

BE A CHEF

Smiling, Mr. Wilson asked, "Now, let me ask you again: who has a superpower?"

ABOUT THE AUTHOR

Christina Dankert is a second-grade teacher. She has a passion for literacy and believes that we can change the world by reading to the children in our lives. This is her debut picture book.

She lives in Sylvania, Ohio, with her husband, Chad, and their two children. She has dreamed of collaborating with her husband to merge their two professions of educator and artist into one meaningful product. The Kindness Machine allowed that dream to come true. Learn more about Christina at www.christinadankert.com.

ABOUT THE ILLUSTRATOR

Chad Dankert is a creative director and storyteller. As a child, he grew up doodling on all of his papers in school. Similar to Mr. Wilson, he believes design, art, and creativity can help engage people and bring them together in meaningful ways, and that anyone can learn to be an artist through practice and patience. This is his debut picture book.